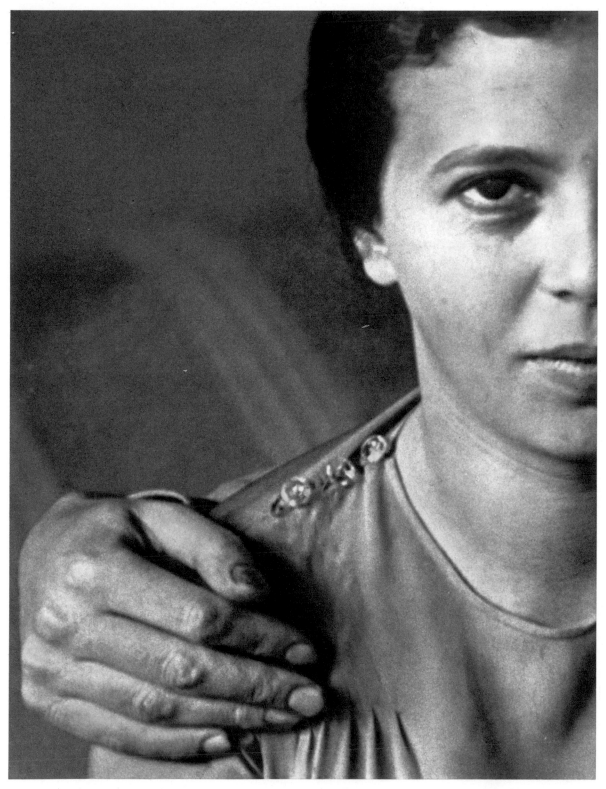

1931

André Kertész

André Kertész

Sixty Years of Photography

1912-1972

edited by Nicolas Ducrot

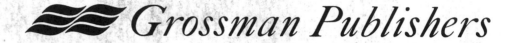 Grossman Publishers

New York

1972

To Elizabeth

Acknowledgments

The author wishes to express his appreciation to Elizabeth Kertesz for her faith and partnership and to Nicolas Ducrot for his understanding and spiritual communion during the preparation of this book.

COPYRIGHT 1972 IN ALL COUNTRIES
OF THE
INTERNATIONAL COPYRIGHT UNION
BY
ANDRE KERTESZ

ALL RIGHTS RESERVED

FIRST PUBLISHED IN 1972 BY
GROSSMAN PUBLISHERS
625 MADISON AVENUE, NEW YORK,
N.Y. 10022

PUBLISHED SIMULTANEOUSLY
IN CANADA BY
FITZHENRY AND WHITESIDE, LTD.

SBN 670-12385-4

LIBRARY OF CONGRESS
CATALOGUE CARD NUMBER: 72-77700

PRINTED IN FRANCE BY
BRAUN-MULHOUSE-FRANCE

1933

Brother Seeing-Eye

Paul Dermée, the Dadaiste poet, wrote this poem as a preface to the catalogue for André Kertész' first one-man show at the gallery Sacre du Printemps in Paris in 1927. At the time, the Dadaists were handing out little stickers on which was written:

"You who do not see, please think of those who can."

The title is an allusion to a 13th century home for blind friars and beggars where the monk in charge, the only man with sight, was named: "Brother Seeing-Eye."

If only for the rhyme, Hamlet, you had to add:
There is more in nature than in works of art and literature!
Only discoverers and inventors create, enriching the public domain. It exists only through them, for which they are given grudging thanks.
To make continuous discoveries in the visual world one need only look with eyes whose retinas, with each blink, become virgin again—film endlessly unwinding.
All of you, do you not photograph nature on a plate that you have not changed since the day you were born!

Kertész,

Eyes of a child whose every look is the first,
which see the Emperor naked when he is clothed in lies;
which take fright at the canvas-draped phantoms haunting the quais of the Seine;
which marvel at the all-new pictures that create, without malice, three chairs in the sun of the Luxembourg Garden, Mondrian's door opening onto the stairs, eyeglasses thrown on a table beside a pipe.
No rearranging, no posing, no gimmicks, nor fakery.
Your technique is as honest, as incorruptible, as your vision.
In our home for the blind,
Kertész is a Brother Seeing-Eye

Translated by Nicolas-Olivier McGinley

Paul Dermée

CHRONOLOGY

1894
Born July 2, Budapest, Hungary.
1912
Baccalaureate from the Academy of Commerce, Budapest.
Employed as a clerk in the Budapest Stock Exchange.
Buys his first camera (an ICA box camera using 4.5×6 cm plates) and begins shooting candid street scenes, genre subjects.
1913
Buys a new camera, ICA Bebe (4.5×6 cm plates).
1914–1918
Serves in the Austro-Hungarian army. Wounded in 1915. Photographs the war and the Commune as an amateur with Goërz Tenax (4.5 × 6 cm plates).
1916
Receives prize for satiric self-portrait from *Borsszem Jankó* magazine.
1917
First published photos in *Erdekes Ujsag* magazine (March 25; first cover June 26, 1925).
1925
Moves to Paris.
1925–1928
Does free-lance reportage for the *Frankfurter illustrierte*,
UHU magazine, *Berliner illustrierte, Strasburger illustrierte, Le Nazionale di Fiorenze*, London *Times*, etc.
1927
One-man show, at Sacre du Printemps gallery, March 12.
1928
Buys his first Leica.
Selected to exhibit in the First Independent Salon of Photography.
Vu, edited by Lucien Vogel, begins publication; Kertesz is a major contributor.
1929
His photographs are purchased for the collections of the Staatliche Museen Kunstbibliothek, Berlin, and the Konig-Albert Museum, Zwickau.
1930
Art et Médecine begins publication; Kertesz is a major contributor until 1936.
Is awarded a silver medal at the *Exposition Coloniale*.
1932
Thirty-five prints in the exhibition of modern European photography at the Julien Levy Gallery, New York.
1933
Marries Elizabeth Sali.
Enfants, with text by Jaboune, is published.
1934
Group show at Leleu's, the noted decorator.
Group show at Galerie de la Pléiade, Paris.
Paris Vu par André Kertesz, with text by Pierre MacOrlan, is published.
1936
Nos Amis les Bêtes, with text by Jaboune, is published.
October: Arrives in New York, under contract with Keystone Studios.
1937
Les Cathédrales du Vin, with text by Pierre Hamp, is published in Paris.
Terminates contract with Keystone Studios.
1937–1949
Free-lances for *Harper's Bazaar, Vogue, Town and Country, the American Magazine, Collier's, Coronet, Look.*
1944
Becomes an American citizen.
1945
Day of Paris, with text by George Davis, is published.
1946
One-man show at the Art Institute of Chicago.
1949
Signs exclusive contract with Condé Nast Publications.

1962
Terminates contract with Condé Nast Publications.
One-man show at Long Island University, New York.
1963
Is awarded a gold medal at the IV Mostra Biennale Internazionale della Fotografia, Venice, Italy.
One-man show at the Bibliothèque Nationale, Paris.
1964–1965
André Kertesz, Photographer, with text by J. Szarkowski, is published.

One-man show at the Museum of Modern Art, New York.
1965
Appointed honorary member of A.S.M.P.
Guest of Honor at the Miami Conference on Communication Arts, University of Miami, Coral Gables, Florida.
1967
Participates in the group show "The Concerned Photographer" at the Riverside Museum, New York.
1968–1969
"The Concerned Photographer" in Matsuya, Tokyo.

1970
Exhibits ten photographs at the U.S. Pavilion at the World's Fair Expo 1970, Tokyo, Japan.
1971
One-man show at the Moderna Museet, Stockholm.
One-man show at the Magyar Nemzeti Galeria Budapest, Hungary.
On Reading is published.
1972
One-man show at Valokuvamuseon, Helsinki, Finland.

ARTICLES ABOUT ANDRE KERTESZ

Pierre MacOrlan. "La photographie et le fantastique social." *Les Annales*, Paris, March 1927.
Criticism of the exhibition at Sacre du Printemps gallery. *Comoedia*, March 12, 1927, Paris.
Montpar. "Photo Kertész." *Chantecler*, March 19, 1927.
Pierre MacOrlan. "L'Art littéraire d'imagination et la photographie." *Les Nouvelles littéraires, artistiques et scientifiques*, No. 37, 1928.
Pierre Bost. "Le Salon des Indépendants de la Photographie." *La Revue hebdomadaire et son supplément illustré*, No. 24, 1928.
Jean Gallotti. "La Photographie, est-elle un art? Kertész." *L'Art vivant*, March 1, 1929.
Jean Vidal. "En photographiant les photographes." Interview with Kertész. *L'Intransigeant*, April 1, 1930.
Carlo Rim. "Défense et illustration de la photographie." *Vu*, Paris, April 20, 1932.
Betrand Guégan. "Kertész et son miroir." *Arts et Métiers graphiques*, No. 37, 1933.
Carlo Rim. "Grandeur et servitude du reporter photographe." *Marianne*, Paris, February 21, 1934.
Pierre Malo. Criticism of the exhibition of photographers at Galerie de la Pléiade. *L'Homme libre*, Paris, November 20, 1934.
Alexander King. "Are Editors Vandals?" *Minicam*, 1939.
Arthur Browning. "Paradox of a Distortionist." *Minicam*, 1939.
John Adam Knight. "Photography." *New York Post*, December 31, 1942.
Maria Giovanna Eisner. "Citizen Kertész." *Minicam*, No. 10, 1944.
Bruce Downes. "André Kertész. Day of Paris." *Popular Photography*, No. 6, 1945.
——. "Day of Paris." *Minicam*, No. 10, 1945.
Elliot Paul. "A Mood from the Dim Past." *Saturday Review of Literature*, March 19, 1945.
William Houseman. "André Kertész." *Infinity*, No. 4, 1959.
Carol Schwalberg. "André Kertész, Unsung Pioneer." *U.S. Camera*, January 1963.

François Pluchart. "Un grand photographe: André Kertész." *Combat Paris*, November 16, 1963.
Brassaï. "My Friend André Kertész." *Camera*, No. 4, 1963.
Greistan Press. "Caricatures and Distortions." *Encylopedia of Photography*.
Maximilian Gautier. "Quand l'oeil a du génie." *Les Nouvelles littéraires*, November 28, 1963.
B. Girod de l'Ain. "André Kertész." *Le Monde*, November 29, 1963.
Alice Gambier. "André Kertész—Photographies." Bibliothèque Nationale, Paris.
George Regnier. "Un long regard amical à André Kertész." *Le Photographe*, December 20, 1963.
Tarcai Bela. "Fotofortenet André Kertész." *Fenykep Muveszeti Tajekoztato*, 1964. III-I.
Robert Kotlowitz. "A Great Photographer Has Spent a Lifetime in Pursuit of His Art." *Show*, March 1964.
L. Fritz Gruber. "André Kertész ein keinesfalls verschollener Altmeister." *Foto Magazin*, July 1964.
Anna Farava. *André Kertész*—Photographic series, Grossman Publishers, New York.
L. Fritz Gruber. "Die Gabel." *Die Welt*, July 3, 1964.
Anatole Jakowsky. "Le Royaume enchanté des naifs." *Beaux Arts*, October 7, 1964.
David Vestal. "André Kertész, Photographer." *Contemporary Photographer*, November 1964–1965.
Margaret R. Weiss. "André Kertész, Photographer." *Saturday Review*, December 20, 1964.
Beaumont Newhall. "*History of Photography: 1830 to the Present Day*." Dist. by N.Y.G.S. Museum of Modern Art.
François Pluchart. "Une définition du langage photographique." *Combat*, December 24, 1964.
"André Kertész—Originator." *Photography*, March 1965.
Dan Budnik. "A point de vue." *Infinity*, March 1965.
Recension of catalogue and exhibition at the Museum of Modern Art in New York. *Times*, London, March 25, 1965.
Ursula Czartoryska, "A Magyar Fotografia Mesterei," *Foto*, November 1965.

L. Fritz Gruber. "André Kertész, a un Piccolo Maestro," *Foto Magazin*, November 1965, Como, Italy.
ASMP Bulletin, November 1965. Report of Kertész's appointment as a member of honor.
Robert E. Hood. "André Kertész, Soldier and Candid Cameraman in World War I." *12 at War*, 1967.
Peter Pollack. *Picture History of Photography*. Abrams Publishers, 1968.
Bill Jay. "A. Kertész, Nude Distortion, an Incredible Experiment." *Creative Camera*, January 1969.
Bill Jay. "A. Kertesz, a Meeting of Friends." *Creative Camera*, August 1969.
Geoffrey James. "André Kertesz." *Vie des Arts*, No. Hiver 1969–1970.
——. "Major Portfolio." *Creative Camera*, September 1969.
Prisma Encyclopedie de la Photographie, Paris, 1970.
Frederick von Almete. "Descriptive Tradition." *Boston after Dark*, April 1, 1970.
Joseph Foldes. "To Become a Photographer." *Popular Photography*, March 1971.
Janet Malcolm. "On and Off the Avenue. *The New Yorker*, May 1, 1971.
Kurt Bergengen. "For alla med Kamera: André Kertész." *Aftonbladet*, May 1971.
Margaret R. Weiss. "Everyman's Reader." *Saturday Review*, July 3, 1971.
Manuel Glasser. "Portfolio Kertesz: Paris um 1930." *Du*, July 1971.
Zay Laslo. "Az Ember A Kep Es A Muveszet." *Foto*, No. 6, 1971.
"Ein Pioner der Fotografie und ihrer hochsten Vollender: André Kertész." *Die Welt*. September, 1971.
Bozoky-Maria. "André Kertesz." *Fotomuveszet*, November 20, 1971.
"Les Nus Etranges d'André Kertesz." *Photo Magazine*, March 1972.

NOTES TO THE PLATES

Half-Title Elizabeth, Paris, 1931
Title Page AZ EST, Budapest, April 27, 1920
Copyright The Duck, Savoie, 1933
7 Behind Notre-Dame, October 1925, Paris
9 My mother's hands, 1919, Budapest
10 Spring shower, 1921, Budapest

11 Hazy day, November 1920, Budapest
12 Ripples, May 11, 1913, Hungary
13 April snow, April 13, 1913, Budapest
14 Iskola Ter, February 19, 1920, Budapest
15 Downtown Esztergom, February 1, 1917, Hungary
16 Boskay Ter, 1914, Budapest

17 Rákos Patak, 1914, Hungary
18 Torok—Balint, August 19, 1922, Hungary
19 Tisza—Szalka, July 6, 1924, Hungary
20 HoldVilág Utca, May 9, 1916, Hungary
21 Cock fight, February 19, 1920, Hungary
22 Accordionist, October 21, 1916, Esztergom

23 Wandering violinist, July 19, 1921, Abony, Hungary
24 Village Madonna, September 26, 1920, Sziget-Becse
25 The swing, September 26, 1917, Esztergom
26–27 Gypsy children, November 10, 1916, and June 27, 1917, Esztergom
28 Little geese, April 24, 1918, Esztergom
29 Friends, September 3, 1917, Esztergom
30 Reading, 1915, Esztergom
31 The slide, March 2, 1916, Pozsony
32 At the puppet show, May 19, 1920, Budapest
33 Circus, May 19, 1920, Budapest
34 Boy sleeping, May 25, 1912, Budapest
35 Lovers, May 15, 1915, Budapest
36 Lagymanyos, October 7, 1920, Budapest
37 Sunset, May 15, 1917, Esztergom
38–39 Duna Haraszti, May 30, 1920, Hungary
40 Swimming, September 14, 1919, Duna Haraszti
41 Underwater Swimmer, August 31, 1917, Esztergom
42 Zebegeny, May 2, 1915, Hungary
43 Soccer players, August 1917, Esztergom
44 Waiting for the ship, May 20, 1919, Budapest
45 Marburg, July 12, 1917, Austria
46 Pomaz, June 11, 1916, Hungary
47 Batorkeszi, September 29, 1916, Hungary
48 Trio, May 6, 1923, Raczkeve
49 The drafted gypsy, October 23, 1916, Esztergom
50 Budafok, 1919, Hungary
51 Sunday afternoon, June 1919, Duna Haraszti
52 Hungarian landscape, 1914, Puszta
53 Plowing, April 2, 1917, Esztergom
54 Working in the field, September 19, 1924, Tisza Szalka
55 Country accident, September 1916, Esztergom
56 An old woman, June 30, 1919, Sziget Becse
57 Small-town judge, September 29, 1916, Batorkeszi
58 Tender touch, August 10, 1915, Bilinski
59 Mobilization, July 28, 1914, Budapest
60 Writing home, September 26, 1916, Esztergom
61 Gorz, January 1, 1915 (Austria now Italy)
62 Gologory, July 22, 1915, Poland
63 Turkish troops leaving on board of the *Minna Horn*, last ship to depart, July 26, 1918, Braila, Rumania
64 Transport, October 19, 1918, Braila, Rumania
65 Officer being stripped of his badges, at the beginning of the Commune, March 21, 1919, Budapest
66 Going home, October 1918, Brasso, Transylvania
67 A Red Hussar leaving, June 1919, Budapest
68 Forced march to the front, between Lonié and Mitulen, July 19, 1915, Poland
70 Satiric dancer, 1926, Paris
71 Distortion portrait, 1927, Paris
72 Distortion #60, 1933, Paris
73 Distortion #6, 1933, Paris
74 Distortion #159, 1933, Paris
75 Distortion #40, 1933, Paris
76 Study, May 17, 1941, New York
77 Study nude, December 26, 1939, New York
78 Melancholic Tulip, February 10, 1939, New York
79 Colette, 1930, Paris
80 Comtesse Michael Karolyi, 1927, Paris
81 Noemi Ferenczi, 1926, Paris
82 Miss Johnson, 1927, Paris
83 Eisenstein, 1929, Paris
84 In the late Emanuel Gondouin's studio: Lipchitz, Giacometti, and Delaunay sitting, 1934, Paris
85 Left: Marie Laurencin, 1930; right: Louis Tihanyi, 1926, Paris
86 Tihanyi, Café du Dôme, 1925, Paris

87 Brancusi, 1928, Paris
88 Left: Jean Lurçat, 1929; above right: Comtesse de Noailles, 1931; below, right: André Bauchant, 1928
89 Miss Gunvor Berg, 1926, Paris
90 Left: Foujita, 1928, Paris; right: Noguchi, June 6, 1945, New York
91 Chagall and his family, 1933, Paris
92 Rue Delambre, 1929, Paris
93 Maurice Vlaminck, 1928, Paris
94 Left: One and a half Monsieur Aguet, 1927; right: Jean A. Ducrot and Bubu, 1928, Paris
95 Paul Dermée, Prampolini and Seuphor, 1927, Paris
96 Charles Maurras at the "Action Française," 1928, Paris
97 Self-portrait, 1927, Paris
98 Picture hanging, 1928, Paris
99 At the Bobino, 1932, Paris
100 Broken plate, 1929, Paris
101 Tristan Tzara, 1926, Paris
102 Alexander Calder, 1929, Paris
103 "Fete Foraine," 1931, Paris
104 "Bistro," 1927, Paris
105 After the ball, 1926, Paris
106 Pierre MacOrlan, 1927, Paris
107 "Bal Musette," 1926, Paris
108 Wooden horses, 1929, Paris
109 Tuileries Garden, 1928, Paris
110 The puppy, 1928, Paris
111 Luxembourg Garden, 1928, Paris
112 Shadows, 1931, Paris
113 Ernest, 1931, Paris
114–15 Chairs of Paris, 1927, 1929, Paris
116 Mondrian's glasses and pipe, 1926, Paris
117 Fork, 1928, Paris
118 Piet Mondrian in his studio, 1926, Paris
119 Chez Mondrian, 1926, Paris
120 Cello study, 1926, Paris
121 Quatuor, 1926, Paris
122 "Attelage," 1925, Paris
123 "Aux Halles," 1928, Paris
124 Street scene, 1928, Paris
125 Montparnasse, 1928, Paris
126 Rue Vavin, 1925, Paris
127 Window, 1928, Paris
128 "Sécurité," 1927, Paris
129 Dubo, Dubon, Dubonnet, 1934, Paris
130 On the quais, 1926, Paris
131 Siesta, 1927, Paris
132 Alone, 1931, Paris
133 Sidewalk, 1929, Paris
134 Noontime, 1929, Paris
135 Fishing, 1929, Paris
136 Pont des Arts, 1932, Paris
137 Eiffel Tower, 1929, Paris
138 Carrefour, 1930, Blois
139 Evening square, 1927, Paris
140 Place Gambetta, 1929, Paris
141 1928, Meudon
142 Sheep, May 1, 1931, Paris
143 Prize winner, May 1, 1931, Paris
144–45 At the Bourse, 1926, Paris
146–47 Market day, 1928, Megeve, Savoy
148–49 Fallen horse, 1927, Paris
150 Telephone wires, 1927, Paris
151 Fishing boats, 1929, Dunkerque
152 Window dressing, 1925, Paris
153 "Something interesting," 1930
154–55 Legs—1928, 1927, 1925, 1939

156 In a bistro, 1927, Paris
157 Shaving, 1930, Paris
158 Hospital ward, 1929, Blois
159 Father Lambert, 1928, France
160 Dourdan, 1931, Ile de France
161 1929, Pontoise
162 Piana, 1932, Corsica
163 Angel, 1928, Chartre
164 In the cloister, 1928, Soligny-sur-Orne
165 In the cellar, 1948, Williamsburg
166 Lost cloud, 1937, New York
167 Puddle, September 17, 1967, New York
168 Wall Street canyon, November 21, 1965
169 Pigeons, November 15, 1971
170 Around St. Vincent's Hospital, November 15, 1971
171 Brick walls, October 23, 1961
172 Newtown, October 5, 1958, Connecticut
173 Sziget Becse, June 1971, Hungary
174 Tudor City, August 25, 1962
175 Imre, 1948, Budapest
176 Ballet, 1938, New York
177 Lake Mohonk, September 27, 1970
178 Water tower, December 1, 1962
179 Fan, December 1937
180 Winter garden, December 23, 1970
181 Washington Square, January 9, 1954
182 Homing ship, October 13, 1944
183 Akron, April 19, 1947, Ohio
184 The Heron, April 26, 1969, New York
185 "Buy," November 15, 1962, Long Island University
186 Promenade, October 17, 1962, New York
187 The white horse, October 17, 1962
188 Granada, June 1971, Spain
189 Empty room, June 28, 1948, New York
190 Disappearing act, August 29, 1955, New York
191 Thomas Jefferson, March 8, 1961, Utica
192 Creator, June 4, 1959, New York
193 Sixth Avenue, April 28, 1959, New York
194 Street singer, April 13, 1969, New York
195 Corridor, 1947, New York
196 Sunday in Washington Square, September 28, 1969
197 Exhibition, October 29, 1967, New York
198 Loneliness, June 19, 1966, New York
199 Acapulco, 1952, Mexico
200 Rainy day, September 14, 1968, Tokyo
201 Hand play, September 22, 1968, Tokyo
202 Broken bench, September 20, 1962, New York
203 The lecturer, March 28, 1969, New York
204 Manchester, September 15, 1946, Vermont
205 Twilight, June 1937, Vermont
206 Sopron, June 1971, Hungary
207 Landing Pigeon, March 2, 1960, New York
208 Mount Kisco, October 30, 1959, New York
209 Armonk, 1941, New York
210 Peggy Guggenheim, September 20, 1945, New York
211 Still life with snake, June 12, 1960, New York
212 Rencontre, May 8, 1959, Texas
213 Buenos Aires, September 17, 1962, Argentina
214–15 Three September windows, 1970, New York
216 & 217 Rinson de la Victoria, June 1971, Malaga, Spain
218 Southport, August 14, 1949, Long Island
219 Christopher Street, May 1950, New York
220 Meiji Shrine, September 18, 1968, Tokyo, Japan
221 Nara, October 8, 1968, Japan
222 Museum of Modern Art, 1964, New York
223 "No Title," October 22, 1959, New York
224 January 1, 1972, Martinique

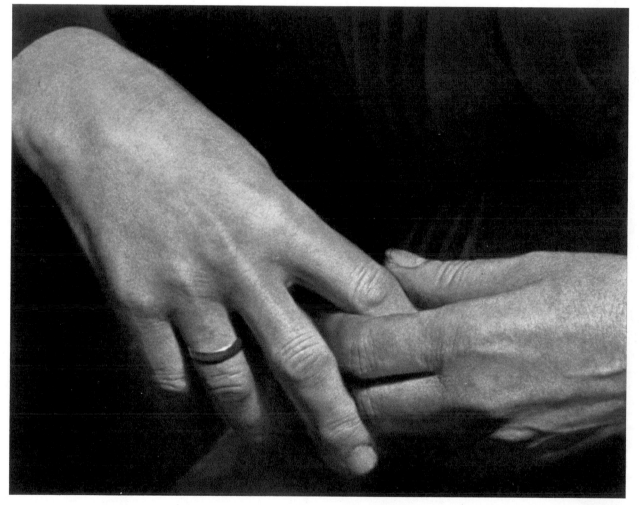

1919

1921

1920

1913

1920

14

1917

1914

1914

1924

19

1920

1916

1921

1920

1917

25

1916

1917

1918

1917

1915

1916

1920

1920

1912

34

1915

1920

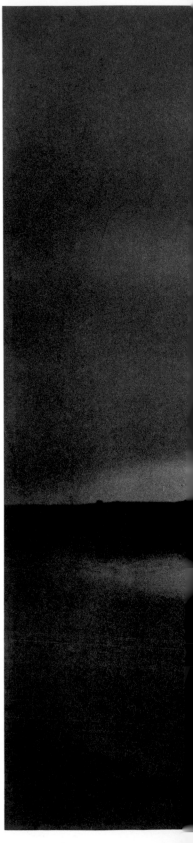

1917

36

1920

1919

1917

1915

42

1917

43

1919

1917

1916

1916

1923

1916

1919

1919

51

1914

1917

1924

1919

1916

1915

1914

191

1915

1915

1918

1919

1918

1919

1915

1926

1927

1933

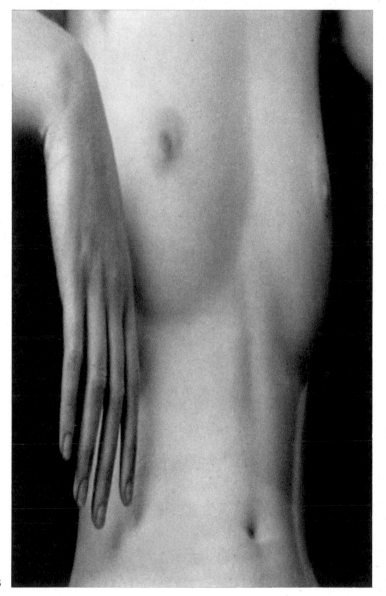

1933

1933

74

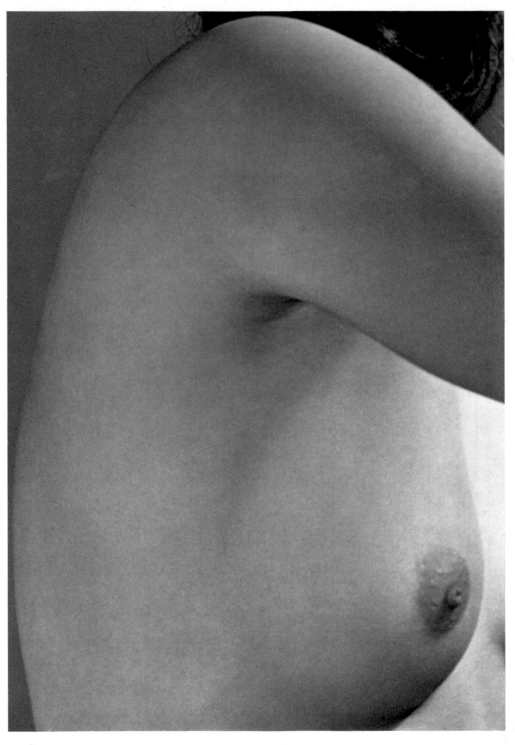

1941

76

1939

1939

1930

1926

1927

1929

19

1930

1926

1928

1931

1929

192

88

1926

1928

1945

1929

1928

1927

1928

1927

1927

1928

1932

19

1926

1929

1931

1927

1927

1929

1928

1931

1931

1927

1927

1929

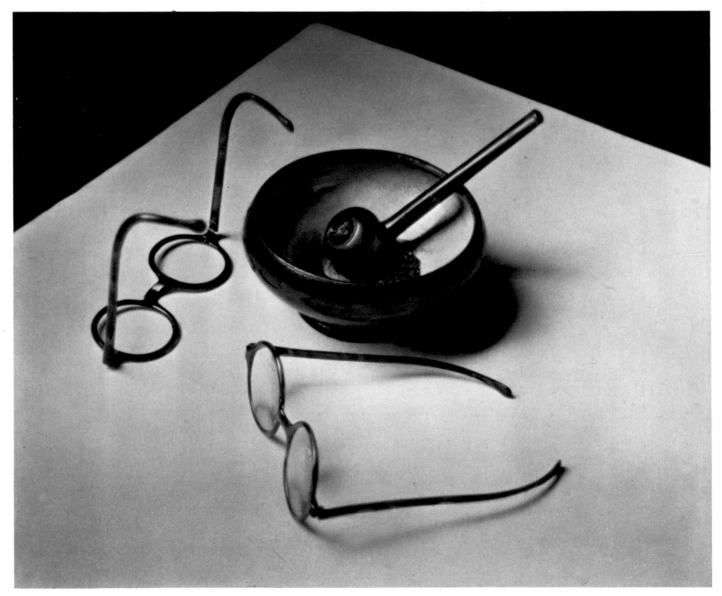

1926

1928

1926

1926

119

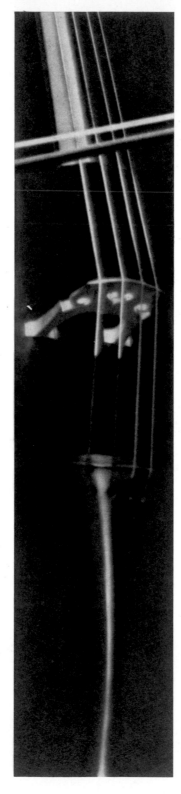

1926

1925

122

1928

1928

1928

1925

1928

1927

1934

1926

1927

19

1929

1929

1932

1929

137

1927

1929

1928

1931

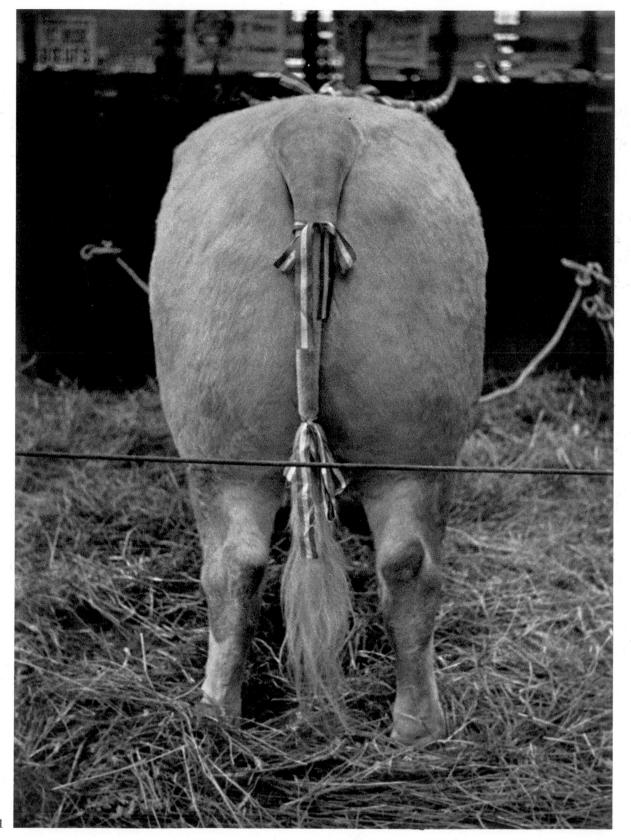

1931

1926

1928

1927

1927

1925

152

1930

1928

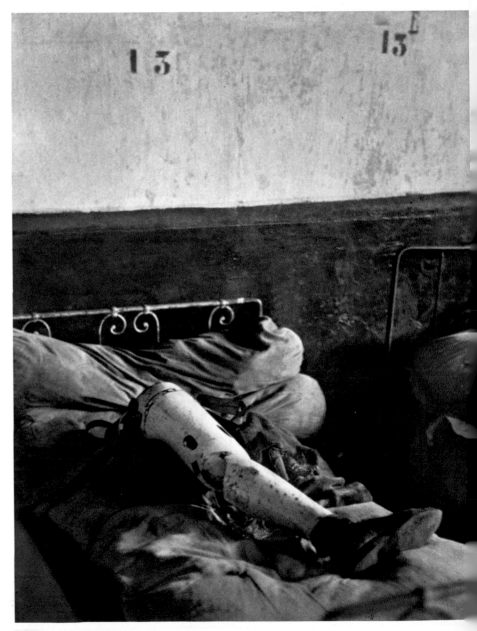

1927

925

1939

1927

1930

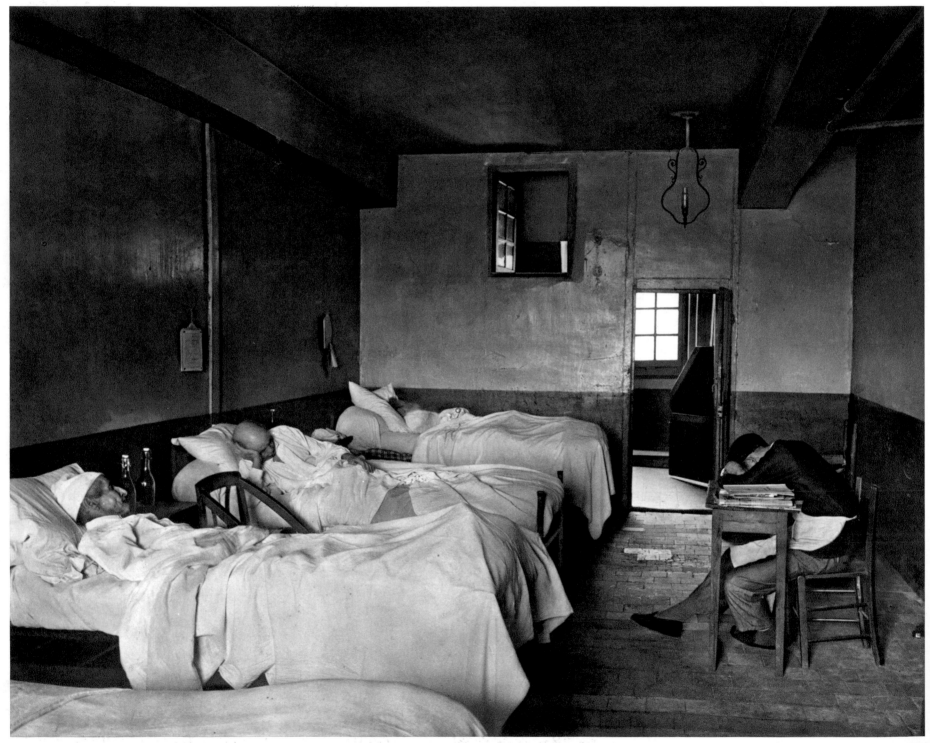

1929

1928

1931

1929

1

1928

1928

1948

1937

1967

1965

1971

1961

19

1971

1962

1948

175

1962

1937

19

1954

1944

1947

1969

1962

1962

1962

1971

1948

1959

1959

193

19

1947

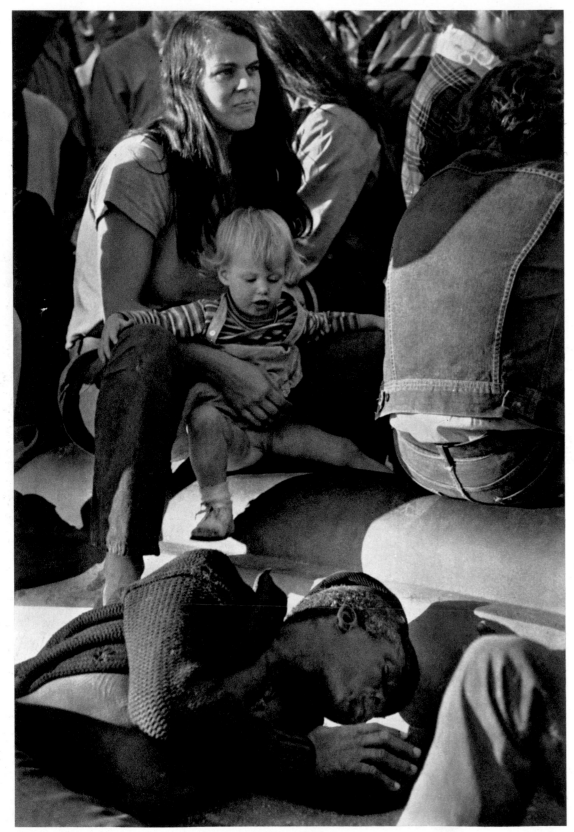

1969

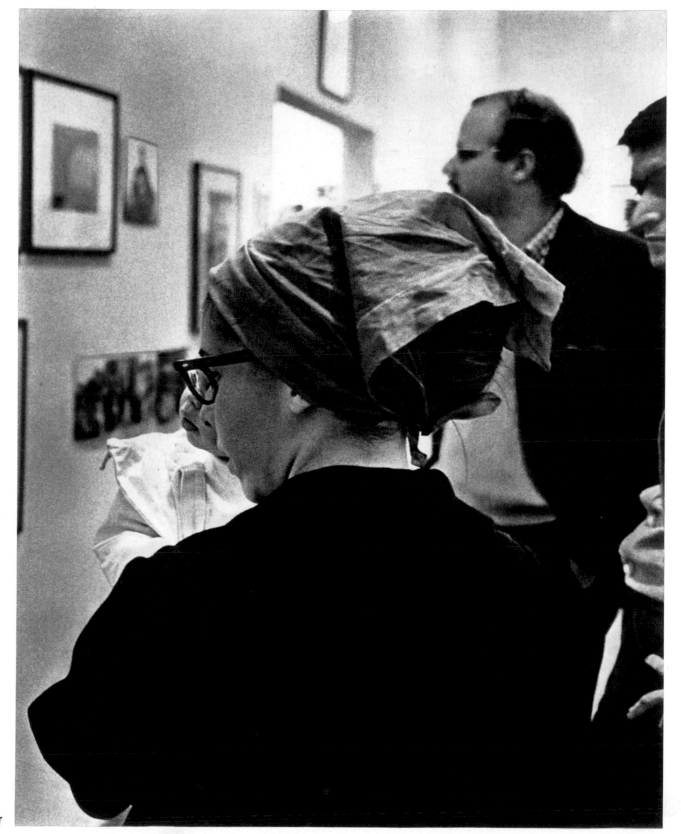

1967

1966

1952

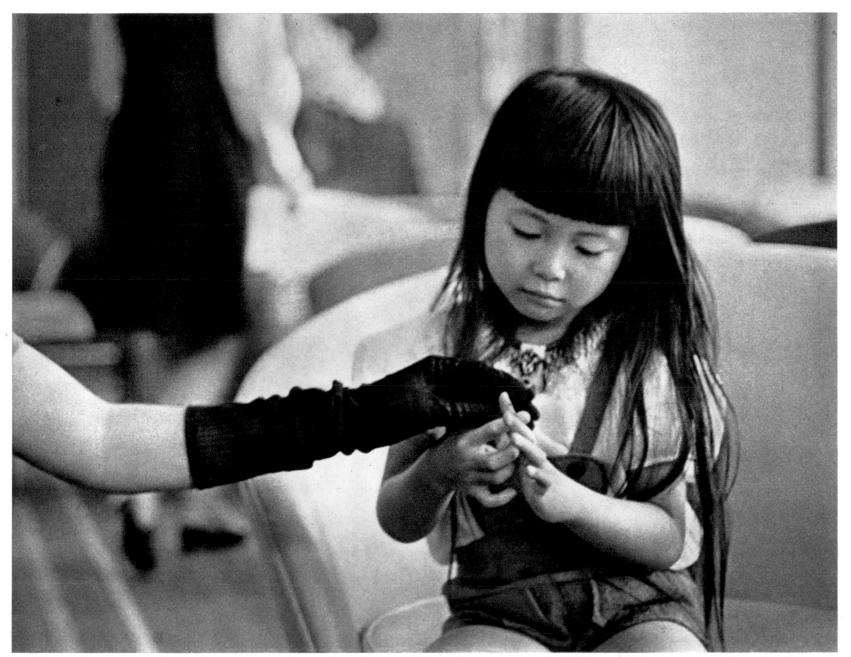

1968

1962

1946

1937

19

1960

1959

1941

1945

1960

1959

1970

1970

1970

1971

1971

1971

1949

1950

1968

1968

1964

1959

1972